A Praising Heart

A Praising Heart

Poems to His Glory

JOANNA NICOL

A Praising Heart
Published by Joanna Nicol
with Castle Publishing Ltd
New Zealand

© 2021 Joanna Nicol

ISBN 978-0-473-56921-1 (Softcover)

Production & Typesetting:
Andrew Killick
Castle Publishing Services
www.castlepublishing.co.nz

Internal Design:
Joanna Nicol

Cover Design:
Paul Smith

ALL RIGHTS RESERVED

No part of this publication may be reproduced,
stored in a retrieval system, or transmitted
in any form or by any means, electronic, mechanical,
photocopying, recording or otherwise,
without prior written permission from the author.

Contents

Introduction	7
In the Beginning	8
A Prayer for the Day	9
African Eden	10
For God So Loved the World	12
The Ladybird	13
Three Haiku	14
Three Haiku	15
Exhortation to the Body of Christ	16
Confession	18
Beautiful Jesus	19
Lo! I Am With You Always	20
A Prayer to the Lord	21
Praise the Lord!	22
The Purple Pansy	23
Daily Prayer	24
Come Unto Me	25
I Have Called You	26
Open Your Eyes	28
Judge Not	29
Child of God's Heart	30
Teach Me Thy Way	31
The Joy of Knowing Jesus	32
Wonderful Lord	34
My Heart is Yours	36
Jesus is the One	37
The Haven On the Highway	38

Nuggets	40
Christmas	42
A Prayer at Christmas	43
Winter	44
Spring is Coming	45
Refreshing	46
You Are Coming Again	47
Behold! I Make All Things New	48
You Are God	50
It's All About You Lord	52
Celebrating the Tabernacle of the King	54
The New Jerusalem	55
Messiah King	56
Alphabet of the King	58
Forgiveness	59
True Light	60
The Rider On the White Horse	61
About the Author	62

Introduction

From early childhood days I have always greatly enjoyed the lilt and rhyme of words. I was never happier than being with a good storybook or my *Child's Garden of Verses* by Robert Louis Stevenson.

As a little girl born & brought up on a farm in the highlands of Kenya, East Africa I wrote descriptive poems of scenery and nature. Later as a Latin & French student I gained understanding of the source and formation of words, and delighted in the way that words in my poems often just flowed together. I have come to realise that this is a gift from God.

My mother instilled faith in me as a little child to believe in God. However, it was not until adulthood that I surrendered my life to Jesus Christ, the One True God, the Living Word – the Creator and Giver of natural talents and spiritual gifts.

Everything has a beginning and one of the first things that happened to me with my writing was that more poems honouring and praising God for Who He is began forming and flowing under His direction.

With encouragement from friends to share this collection, *A Praising Heart: Poems to His Glory* has been produced "for such a time as this."

My hope is that you will be inspired and encouraged in the ups and downs of daily life to realise that all things are possible in Jesus Christ, the One True God who wants us all to know Him. He is the answer to our need for inner peace and assurance of eternal life. Make Him Lord of your life today that you may be filled with new joy and blessed hope!

Joanna

In the Beginning

In the Beginning was the Word
The Word was Spirit, the Spirit of God
God the Trinity, Perfect Unity
All manifested in the Word

This Word became for us a Man
The Man was Jesus come down from Heav'n
God's Only Son, the Blessed One
All part of God's Eternal Plan

He came to seek and save the lost
He bore our sins upon the Cross
Humble Saviour, Glorious Lord
Risen in Power, Mighty God!

He's the Victorious, Triumphant King!
He's conquered Death – shouts of praise ring!
Jesus is Lord, Living Word
To Him His saints ever shall sing:

"Lamb of God Whose precious Blood
Has bought for us a place in Heav'n
Jesus our King to You we bring
Our hearts, our lives, our everything

"We reach towards You, God of all Glory
We long to touch You – to see Your face
Glorious Spirit, God Eternal
Come now and bless us, fill this place

"We are Your children, You are our Father
Show us Your mercy, grant us Your peace
You are our life, Lord – we need You always
We bow before You, God of Grace"

Can be sung to the tune of: Morning has Broken

A Prayer for the Day

Oh! Father help me as I pray
To know Your will for me today
To learn how best to please You Lord
And spread the news of You abroad

For I love You Lord and want to do
Things only honourable and true
To love my neighbour as I should
To tell the truth – forsake falsehood

If I can follow in Your Way
Work hard and do my best all day
Then surely I will thankful be
To know Your Spirit lives in me

African Eden

A twig snapped and two eyes engaged mine
The magnificent creature motionless,
I held my breath,
And long moments stretched into Eternity.
With fluid grace the great cat
melted into the long grass...
Pressed against the rock my heart beat again
While the hot sun climbed steadily higher
and hours passed...

Shadows from the umbrella thorn
passed across my face
As heavy galleon clouds sailed in from the West.
Lightning forked and faint thunder
rumbled in the distance...
Isolated raindrops stung my bare skin.
I huddled against the tree-trunk as the torrent fell,
The weaverbirds' nests clung to the branches
while the thirsty earth drank its fill...

The long white thorns glistened
as the sun returned,
Spreading warm gold fingers over the plain.
An ant resumed tugging its load
and the hot earth steamed.
Faintly a cowbell tinkled, the cattle grazing
under the watchful eye of a Masai herdsman.
As the long hot afternoon slipped into early evening
a cool breeze rippled the tawny grass
and shy bushbuck stepped daintily,
ears twitching, tails flicking...

Heading for home a Kavirondo Crane
    honked mournfully while a hawk glided silently,
       gazing intently earthward,
           suddenly dropping like a stone.
Another meal in its claws,
          it rose again into the heavens.
The fingers of the sinking sun
  painted streaks of apricot across the sky
      and darkening shadows spread
        stealthily over the plain.
A rustle in the long grass disturbed my reflection
     and once again a twig snapped…

Two unblinking eyes again met mine,
        the creature had returned…
Warm waves of Love flooded my being,
  my spirit soared, my heart reached out with
  the embrace of the Creator for His creatures,
Transported into a former Eden
  where Man named the animals
     and God the Father smiled
        as He blessed His whole creation,
Where Fear was unknown
     and the Light of Truth shone
       into every shadow.

For God So Loved the World

For God so loved the world that He gave His only Son
That whosoever believeth in Him should not perish,
should not perish, but have everlasting life

And this life is in His Son, this life is in His Son
That the Father may be glorified
In Heaven and here amongst men

And whosoever believeth, and whosoever believeth
In the Name of Jesus Christ the Son
To them the Gift is given

And the Gift is Eternal Life, Eternal Life with God
For we are created to live with Him
In everlasting Love

For God is Love, and this Love is in His Son
Who laid down His life on this earth for us
That in Him we might all become one

For God so loved the world that He gave His only Son
That whosoever believeth in Him should not perish,
should not perish, but have everlasting life

The Ladybird

Inspired by a friend's daughter dressed as a ladybird visiting sick children in hospital & taking surprise gifts. The ladybird is known as the healing insect, keeping flowers and foliage healthy by eating marauding insects in the garden.

    Ladybird bright,
        bringing delight,
    Radiantly smiling,
        you light up our day.
    Tenderly caring,
        surprises sharing,
    Beautiful ladybird,
        please won't you stay?

Lovingly greeting,
    joyfully meeting,
Moving among us
    and holding our hand,
Gently revealing
    the Source of true healing,
Beautiful ladybird,
    you understand.

    As you draw near,
        dispelling our fear,
    Light as of Heaven
        bursts on our soul.
    Laughing and giving
        each moment living,
    Touching our heart
        and making us whole.

Three Haiku
Theme: *Creation*

RAINBOW
Rainbow arc up high
Sign of hope, no more flooding
We sigh in relief

HIGH TIDE
Roaring breakers crash
Limpet clings to rocky crag
Sighing sea recedes

MOWN LAWN
Fresh-smelling cut grass
Garden air pungent sweetness
Sunshine warms the earth

Three Haiku
Theme: *Food for Thought*

ORGANIC
Think what we will eat
Nature's garden best for health
Makes us strong and well

INNER CONTENTMENT
Get rid of all strife
Love our brothers and sisters
Reach out with our love

ETERNITY
Are we all alone?
Universe in suspension
We are very small

Exhortation to the Body of Christ

The Lord our God is doing a new thing in these days
Joyfully lift up your voice
                         and clap your hands in praise
He is pouring out His Spirit on people young and old
Calling men to worship Him and making people bold
His message of salvation and eternal life to tell
Bringing captives freedom
                         that in Jesus they may dwell

The Spirit that He gives to us fills us with new life
Refreshing as a pure clear stream
                         He calms our daily strife
Rejuvenates our flagging steps,
                         restores us from within
And gives us power from on high to conquer daily sin

All thanks and praise and blessing
                         to our Heavenly Father raise
For the wonders and the miracles
                         He's doing in these days
And to His Church on earth which in this place
                         is me and you
He has given power and blessing
                         those same miracles to do

Arise you saints, equip yourselves
                         in heavenly armour bright
Prepare yourselves for battle
                         as true soldiers of the Light
Go forth into the darkness
                         where the devil holds his sway
And rout him with your two-edged Sword
                         for Jesus is the Way

Speak forth the Word of God
                              with fearlessness and truth
Step out upon life's highway
                              with the energy of youth
For God your Father waits for you
                              with Jesus at His side
And angels, they are cheering
                              as they crowd you round beside

Press on to higher glory
                              reaching forward for the prize
The Crown of Life that Jesus holds
                              and love is in His eyes
As He watches and He intercedes
                              for you along the way
Delighting in your progress
                              to the dawning of that Day

When in the Father's Kingdom we shall all united be
One in mind and Spirit and in perfect harmony
Lifting hands and voices
                              to our great Redeemer's praise
Singing "Glory, glory, glory, God Almighty!"
                              all our days

Confession

I confess dear Father I confess
That I come not in my own righteousness
But clothed in the robes of Your own dear Son
My Saviour and my Lord Jesus Christ

Dear Father in Your Presence now I stand
Washed and saved by the Blood of the Lamb
And my heart overflows with amazement and joy
That You love me just for who and what I am

Abba Father You are Almighty God
You are Jesus, Holy Spirit, Living Word
You have reached down to me
through the Cross at Calvary
And restored me to fellowship with You

Oh! The wonder of it all will never cease
As You pour out on me Your love and peace
Grant to me a willing heart, a vessel set apart
As a channel for Your love and Your grace

Take my heart O Lord and in it grow
Seeds of love that the world may come to know
Through the Love that You pour
from Your everlasting store
That Jesus is Redeemer and Lord

Beautiful Jesus

Jesus You are beautiful
Jesus You are wonderful
Jesus You are mighty
I love You Lord

And I lift up Your Name
For Your Name is great
I lift up Your Name
Jesus my Lord

You are my precious Saviour
You are my blessed Redeemer
I praise and exalt You
Jesus my Lord

And I lift up Your Name
For Your Name is great
I lift up Your Name
Jesus my Lord

You are mighty in Power
You are beautiful in Truth
The fruit of my lips I bring
To worship You my King

And I lift up Your Name
For Your Name is great
How great is Your Name
My Lord and my God!

Lo! I Am With You Always

Lo! I am with you always
Lo! I am with you always
Lo! I am with you always
Even to the end of time

―

Therefore, go in My Name with My blessing
Therefore, go in My Name with My blessing
Therefore, go in My Name with My blessing
I will make you a fisher of men

―

I will make you a reaper and a sower
I will make you a planter of trees *
I will make you the richer for knowing
My grace in the hour of your need

―

For lo! I am with you always
For lo! I am with you always
For lo! I am with you always
Even to the end of time

―

Strong believers, rooted and established in Jesus, becoming "oaks of righteousness" to His glory. (Isaiah 61: 3)

A Prayer to the Lord

Lord of Light shine through our eyes
That people blind to You may see
Clothe us in Your Spirit bright
Keep us glowing with Your Light

Lord of Truth speak through our lips
That men may hear Your Word
Bring our thoughts captive unto You
That speech and song be always true

Lord of Love reign in our hearts
That we may love each other
Move within us to spread around
That same Eternal Love we've found

Lord of Life dwell in our being
That men may come to know You
Make us vital – glowing – true
Living always unto You

Praise the Lord!

Praise the Lord!

Praise, praise the Lord for all that He has done
For all that He is doing and will do
Praise, praise the Lord for the victory we have won
For His Spirit in us tells us what to do

In times of doubt He strengthens us
by faith to share with Him
The feelings that alone we can't dispel
For only when we come to Him
and tell Him of our fears
Will He comfort us and tell us "All is well"

He walks with us and talks with us
to keep us on the Road
He puts His arm around us when we fall
Lovingly He greets us
and rejoicingly He meets us
For He never fails to hear us when we call

He is the Well of Life and Love and our Security
Our Home on earth and in the heavens above
Oh, may we always give Him praise
and thank Him in return
For the mighty blessings from our Lord of Love

The Purple Pansy

Thoughts that inspired this poem:

Three main petals like the Trinity – A golden 'sunburst' heart or centre like an eye – Purple is a royal colour – The larger petals are like the train of His robe, soft and velvety, caressing, so rich in beauty and depth, reflecting our Lord in His glory – A flower of the field – The gold is like a crown, like a sunrise – Subtle, delicate scent – In the midst of our darkness is the glorious light of Christ

Perfect in purity
Vivid and velvety
Rich and royal
With gold for a King

Flower of the field
Invites me to yield
Kneel and behold Him
King of all kings

His is the beauty
Drawing me deeper
"Come to Me, daughter
Come, enter in"

"Drink of My beauty
Gaze on My glory
Child you are precious
Washed free from sin"

The darkness of Calvary
Blazed into brilliance
Jesus is Lord
And now lives within

Daily Prayer

May your day be blessed
May you be led by the Lord
May you be refreshed in the Living Word
May your heart rejoice and your lips sing praise
As you reach out to Jesus to fill your days
As you gratefully thank Him for your salvation
As you praise Him for the wonder
of His highest creation
Made in God's image like Jesus to be
To reign with Him in Eternity
All power and glory and honour to Him
His plan and His purpose all souls to redeem
Dear Lord, we must each enter through Your Cross
Help us to share the Good News with the lost
Thank You, Lord for Your mercy,
Your love and Your grace
You gave us Life when You died in our place

AMEN

Come Unto Me

Inspired by the scripture in Matthew 11: 28 & 29

Come, come unto Me, come, come unto Me
All ye who labour and are heavily laden
Come, come unto Me and I will refresh you
And I will give you rest for your weary souls

Take My yoke upon you and learn, oh learn from Me
For I am gentle and humble in heart
Learn, oh learn from Me

As you lean upon Me and take My yoke upon you
A new joy will spring from deep within you
For My Spirit sets you free

Come, come unto Me, come, come unto Me
All ye who labour and are heavily laden
Come, come unto Me and I will refresh you
And I will give you rest for your weary souls

Take My yoke upon you and learn, oh learn from Me
For My yoke is easy and My burden is light
Learn, oh learn from Me

Come, come unto Me, come, come unto Me
All ye who labour and are heavily laden
Come, come unto Me and I will refresh you
And I will give you rest for your weary souls

I Have Called You

The Call:
I have called you together to be a chosen Band
I have called you to teach you
from My abundant Hand
I have called you to lead you into the hearts of men
I have called you to proclaim to them all that I AM
So follow, I am Jesus the Captain of your Band
Keep your eyes on things above
and learn of what I've planned
As you learn to listen, the more I will reveal
Of My Father's will for you to help
make whole and heal

The harvest-fields are ready, the world is lost and sad
Go forth as My blessed labourers
and make the people glad
Open up your hearts to Me, open up your minds
I want to bless you richly and give you what is Mine
You are My sons and daughters,
each one especially dear
Take courage, I am with you –
you have no cause to fear
For where I am there's peace and joy
and all of Heaven's Light
My power will flow through you
to overcome the darkest night

So follow, I am Jesus your Captain and your King
I am here right in the midst of you
to teach you and to bring
Wisdom, understanding and healing to your mind
The riches of My Kingdom each one of you will find
I have called you together to be a chosen Band
I have called you to teach you
from My abundant Hand
I have called you to lead you into the hearts of men
I have called you to proclaim to them all that I AM!

The Response:
Teach us Lord to follow and obey all Your commands
Teach us how to love You with heart and voice and hands
Fill us with Your Spirit – empowered from above
Build in us Your Kingdom of Faith and Hope and Love
Lord we are Your family created as Your own
You are our Abba Father – yet on a kingly throne
Our hearts and souls cry out for You,
we long to enter in
Have mercy on Your Body Lord
and cleanse us from within

Forgive us Lord our selfish pride
and lack of zeal for You
Replace in us our lost first love – set us on fire anew
Blaze in us Your Spirit until we freely burn
With a passion for You Jesus
and for Your great Return!
Anoint us with Your Spirit, empower us to be
The children of Your Kingdom –
that all the world may see
The love of Jesus flowing from each and every one
That honour, praise and glory be given to the Son

For thus You have ordained it
ever since the world began
The Coming of the Holy One redeeming sinful man
And Lord we know You're coming in glory once again
To take Your rightful place as King eternally to reign
We bow our knee before You,
we acknowledge You are Lord
Jesus Christ, Messiah, Anointed, Holy Word
Awesome and magnificent – our great Creator King
Before You God we offer you our lives, our everything

You have called us together to be a chosen Band
You have called us to teach us
from Your abundant Hand
You have called us to lead us into the hearts of men
You have called us to proclaim to them
You are the Great I AM!

Open Your Eyes

Open your eyes, see the glory of the King!
Lift up your voice and His praises sing
I love You Lord, I will proclaim
Alleluia – I bless Your Name

Lift up your eyes to the Lord in Heaven above
Lift up your eyes to our living Lord of Love
He reigns on high, He is the King
To His feet now your treasure bring

Lift up your heart, this is your gift to Him
This is your treasure, your daily offering
He loves you so, He died for you
On Calvary's Cross He shed His Blood for you

He is the Lord, Son of God, Jesus Christ
He Is the Father's precious Sacrifice
Give honour due, lift high His Name
Lord of all – to You we give acclaim!

Open your eyes, see the glory of the King!
Lift up your voice and His praises sing
I love You Lord, I will proclaim
Alleluia – I bless Your Name

Acknowledgement to Original Song:
Open Your Eyes
Copyright on verses 2, 3 & 4
added to original song

Judge Not

You say "Judge not by appearance"
For You look only upon the heart
Forgive us Lord for judging what we see
We need Your help to set apart
The things that outwardly define
From what is deep inside the soul

We need Your eyes, Your ears, Your love
To look upon our fellow-men & hear their pain
To listen before speaking, to hold in arms of care
Use us, Lord to help make whole again
Restoring dignity, peace and calm
Bringing freedom, hope and renewed joy of living

Lord, You reign enthroned within our hearts
Only You know the thoughts of all
Only You know the way to take
We bend low to hear the Spirit's call
Direct our lives Lord to bring You glory
Bringing in the end-time harvest sheaves

Child of God's Heart

Child of My heart made in My image
I am your Father longing for you
Reaching out, touching, loving, adoring
Watching and waiting, crying for you

I see you sleeping, I see you waking
Child, I am with you all through the day
My heart is aching, feeling and breaking
Knowing how often you turn Me away

There's not a moment I am not with you
I see you searching, questing for Me
Looking and wondering where you will find Me
I hear you saying: "Are You there for me?"

Now by My Spirit, Child, know My Presence
Pouring My glory into your soul
Fears all dispelling, faith now infilling
Feel now My Presence making you whole

Teach Me Thy Way

Inspired by Psalm 25: 4 & 5

Teach me Thy Way O Lord, direct my path
That I may walk uprightly with Thee
Give me Thy counsel Lord, to me impart
The knowledge of Thy will for me
That I may live as Thou wouldst have me live
That I may be what Thou wouldst have me be
That my whole life might exalt and glorify Thee

Teach me Thy Patience Lord, keep me trusting Thee
That Thou art perfecting within me
That same good work O Lord which Thou didst begin
The day I surrendered my life unto Thee
Until that day when we meet face to face
And I shall see the fullness of Thy Grace
For I shall know Thee as even now Thou knowest me

Teach me Thy Wisdom Lord, help me understand
To know Thy Heart and Mind in me
Give me Thy Love O Lord for my fellow man
That I may reach right out and help him see
That in all things Thou art the One True God
That Jesus is the Truth, the Living Word
That in Thy Holy Spirit we are forever free

Fill me with Grace O Lord, fill my heart and soul
That rivers of Life may flow from within me
Stretch out Thine Hand O Lord and make me whole
That I a vessel pure for Thee may be
That Thou mayest work Thy perfect will in me
That I may grow each moment more like Thee
That Thy true Nature be clearly revealed in me

The Joy of Knowing Jesus

Oh Jesus! The joy of knowing
You live in me
Once I was captive Lord
But You have set me free
Free to love and serve You Lord
Free to conquer sin
By Your Holy Spirit power
That dwells within

Oh Jesus! The death You died
On Calvary's Cross for me
Saved me from the power of sin
And gave new life to me
For by Your Resurrection Lord
You have lifted me
Now Your life and strength is mine
And I have liberty

Oh Jesus! The Blood You shed
At Calvary long ago
Daily cleanses me from sin
Washes me as snow
And by Your precious Blood dear Lord
I can approach the Throne
Bold and confident dear Lord
In You and You alone

Oh Jesus! I give You praise
Be in my voice oh Lord
To tell all people of Your love
And spread Your Word abroad
For unconditional love You are
For the whole world You died
That all may have eternal life
And Lord with You abide

Oh Jesus! Our hearts reach out
To touch You living Lord
Come upon us now in power
Fulfil Your promised Word
Send through us Lord Your holy fire
Make us a burning flame
Cause us to rise this very hour
To glorify Your Name

Oh Jesus! Our Great High Priest
Our Prophet, Saviour, King
Accept our sacrifice of praise
Our lives an offering
May we so grow in grace dear Lord
And wisdom from above
That all in us Your face may see
And know the Father's love

Wonderful Lord

Wonderful, wonderful Lord!
Wonderful, wonderful Lord!
Oh how wonderful is my Jesus!
Wonderful, wonderful Lord!

He is the Sovereign Lord,
He is the Sovereign Lord,
Father, Son and Holy Spirit
He is the Sovereign Lord!

On the Cross at Calvary
He died for you and me
He paid the penalty – rose in victory,
Jesus has set us free!

Released from sin and death
Released from all our strife
Jesus has vanquished the power of the enemy
We have Eternal Life!

He now reigns on high,
He is with God above,
He has sent us His Holy Spirit
Wonderful Lord of Love!

He sees all our heart
He knows all our care
He takes all our burdens from us
He is always there!

He is our greatest Friend
Who loves us without end
He never leaves us – He's always with us
Wonderful, wonderful Friend!

We are His hands and His feet
We are the mouthpiece for Christ
He touches others as He moves through us
We're to be 'salt' and 'light'!

He is the Light of the World
He is the Only True God
He's the Life-Giver, He's not the Life-Taker
He is the Living Word!

He is the Almighty God
He is the Lord Jesus Christ
He is the precious Holy Spirit
We are the Body of Christ!

Beautiful, beautiful Lord!
Beautiful, beautiful Lord!
Oh, how beautiful is my Jesus!
Beautiful, beautiful Lord!

My Heart is Yours

Write the truths of Your laws
on my heart, O my God
Come breathe on me Spirit I pray
Let the thoughts of my heart
know the life of Your Word
And cause me to praise You and say –

You are my Lord, there is no other God
You are my joy and my peace
I run in the pathway of Your commands
Upheld by Your love and Your grace

Like a bird I take wing and I rise on the storm
For Your love draws me upward and higher
Through darkness and cloud to the burst of the sun
Where You reign in absolute power

Your kingdom is freedom and laughter and joy
No pain, sin or grief there abound
You are my Sun and my Light and my Star
In You all my treasure is found

Jesus the Name above all other names
The Light of this world and of Heaven
Source of all Truth, Creator and Friend
Unto You all my worship is given

Jesus is the One

Is the hill too high and hard to ascend?
Does the road of toil never come to an end?
Is the valley of heartache too dark and deep?
Is the mountain of trouble too rocky and steep?

Come, sit beside One who will understand
Entrust your burden into His hand
Lean your careworn weary heart on His breast
With Him is eternal peace and rest

Jesus has entered this world of strife
He lived, He loved and laid down His life
God sent His Son to show us the Way
On the Cross He bore our sins away

Oh! Blessed Saviour, Redeemer and Friend
You promise to be with us to the very end
Yours is the never-ending story
It's all about You, Lord of all glory

You reign on high, You overcame the grave
Mankind to redeem and eternally save
Sin and Death vanquished, we are free to sing
Grateful praises to Jesus our King

We love You Lord – You wear the Crown
Spotless and pure You are the One
You are the Pearl of utmost worth
You are the Lord of Heaven and Earth!

The Haven On the Highway

There's a haven on the highway
and I know that Heaven's there
It is seen in loving faces
and felt in arms of care
It is known in joyful worship
and experienced in prayer
For the Spirit of the Lord of Hosts
is ever-present there

Come into the haven
and lay your burdens down
At the feet of Him who loves you
and Who offers you a crown
Of love and joy and hope and peace
and purpose in His will
So cease from all your striving
and let your heart be still

God made you and He longs to have
relationship with you
He alone can turn your life around
and make things bright and new
He reaches out through others
and sends wisdom from above
His purpose is that you may know
there is a God of Love

He came Himself in Jesus
to a world so lost and marred
His lifeblood poured at Calvary
His body bruised and scarred
He took upon Himself our guilt
our fear and all our sin
He knocks upon our stony hearts
and waits to be let in

He agonises with the world:
"Oh hear the Father's call" –
His Holy Spirit seeking out
the hearts of one and all –
"Come unto Me, I love you
I am the Hope that springs
In each new dawn, in each new birth,
In the tiny bird that sings"

"I am Creator, Elohim
the One True God – I AM
I am Jehovah, Adonai
and I have a perfect plan
To bring all people to Myself
and fill them with My love
To know My Presence here on earth
and in the heavens above

"I made each person special
Each one unique to Me
I made each in My image
to reflect the Trinity
Of Father, Son and Holy Ghost
The perfect matchless King
To reign with Me in Heaven
and with the angels sing"

*In that haven on the highway
the sounds of joy abound
The Name of Jesus lifted
as the people dance around
Their treasure is so rich and free
The Spirit of the Lord
Salvation's well is boundless
in the power of His Word!*

Nuggets

Here we are stationed at Nuggets Point
Poised between earth and sky,
The winking light warns mariners
Of dangers as ships draw nigh.

The ocean breaks round the Nuggets 'ring',
White surf during night and day;
Basking seals and seagulls sing
At the edge where the kelp fronds sway.

Oh! I must down to Nuggets Point,
For the lighthouse beckons still;
To the surf's white edge and the rocky ledge
Where the air is warm and still.

But traveller, watch when the southerly blows
And the gale turns surf into foam;
Hang onto the rail, lean into the gale
And make sure you're heading for home!

The keeper's trail winds out to the light
From the tiny house on the hill;
The sides are steep and the sea is deep,
But many there are who still...

Follow the track in the early dawn
When the sun rises out of the sea,
Drawn to the sight of the Nuggets light
That has captivated me.

So, traveller, pause as you stand and gaze
To the far horizon line,
And remember the days of a bygone age
Now lost in the mists of time…

When a keeper's life was lonely and hard
As he toiled in sun and rain
To maintain the light by day and night
For all on the ocean 'main'.

(acknowledgment for the rhythm of this poem to John Masefield, English Poet Laureate, composer of "Sea Fever")

Christmas

Come Son of God born from above
Touch our weary and careworn hearts to love
Lift our eyes up to see You – risen and free
Reigning in glorious majesty
Radiant in beauty, resplendent in light
God of all power and God of all might

Help us to know You, Spirit within
Releasing and healing, conquering sin
Touch our voice, touch our will
Raise us up to proclaim
Redemption and victory in Jesus' Name!

Move us by love Your purpose to meet
To reach out to others, touch our hands and our feet
Open the windows and doors of our soul
Help us bring peace, to pray and make whole
Hearts that are hurting, sick bodies to heal
Move through us Lord that You may be real

To skeptics and sinners, the rejected, the lost
May the beauty of Jesus shine through the Cross
Where, Lord of Humility, You bled and died
All souls to redeem and with You abide
Touch our hearts, touch our lives, revive us again
Spirit of Truth come now and reign

Fill us with wonder, with praise for our King
Help us touch others that their souls may sing
That they too will bow and Lord You adore
For it's all about You and Your treasure-store
Of endless provision and answers to need
Of assurance and blessing hungry souls to feed

Lord of Eternity, Lord from Above
Touch us anew with the power of Your love

A Prayer at Christmas

Every day I think of you
Every day I pray for you
That God will undertake for you
That God will smooth the way for you
That His Holy Spirit be alive in you
That you will hear His voice each day
That you will praise and pray each day
That you will know His love deep down
And in your heart Lord Jesus crown
That He be first in everything
And cause your soul to worship Him
For life is all about His Presence
Not Christmas Trees and Christmas Presents
There's nothing wrong with those at all
As long as He is Lord of all
May your day be rich in knowing
Your love for Him is ever growing
Be set free from earthly treasure
Feeling deep His Spirit's measure
This priceless Gift the Father gives
That mankind's soul may ever live
Help us Lord to live and be
Honest witnesses for Thee

Winter

Softly and silently Winter's fingers spread the snow
Along bare branches of stark trees below
Mountain-tops gleamed white as the moon arose
Clouds dispersed, stars twinkled
And the hard earth froze

Morning sunlight kissed the crisp, white frost
Around the frozen lake with lines criss-crossed
As early morning skaters whirled and twirled
Scarves flying, revelling in the wintry world

Sleepy children tumbled out of bed
Rushed to the window and downstairs sped
To join the winter revellers with cries of glee
Shouting to each other to come and see

"Look at my snowman! Mine's the best!"
Friendly rivalry for the best-dressed
Snowballs flying as they trudged to school
Reluctant to come under discipline's rule

Dripping branches in the afternoon
Revealed the snowmelt all too soon
The winter's day drew near its close
Sun set, a chilly wind arose

Another frost, more snow and ice now laid
By Winter's fingers – glittering stars soon fade
Cold cloud descends, the night is chill
Earth hard as iron, the air all still

Spring is Coming

Winter chill, fireside glow
Curtains drawn, outside the snow
Hottie-bottle on my feet
Cat beside me, curled up neat
Crackling logs, soup on stove
Cheery company, hearts of love
Keep the snow and ice away
Till the dawning of Spring day
Sunshine melts the dripping snow
Gone the fireside's cheerful glow
Busy workers on the roads
Trucks with honking horns and loads
Mis-shaped snowmen melt away
Slushy pools where once they lay
Spring is coming, Winter's going
Soon it will be time for sowing
Tulip bulbs and daffodils
Crocus and narcissus frills
Colours bright where once was white
Winter's faded out of sight

Refreshing

Golden sand beneath my toes
Water sparkling, sunshine-dappled
Greens and blues in depths unseen
Islands scattered in between

Far horizons draw my gaze
Ocean-liners, fishing-boats
Are but specks and dots in view
Scattered on the ocean blue

Sandworms, driftwood,
              pumice, stones
Seaweed on the tideline
Seas recede with tumbling shells
Drawn to ocean's mighty swells

Small humanity, endless ocean
'Calm' smiles tranquilly on me
Here where beach and ocean meet
Crunching sand beneath my feet

No longer tense and burden-stressed
    Striding forward, weights all gone
        I breathe in deep the fresh salt air
            Refreshed again, released from care

You Are Coming Again

Awaiting and desiring for Your Return Lord
Longing for Your Appearing, Living Word
People despair and lives are torn apart
Only You can mend Earth's broken heart

Come, flood us again with Your Holy Spirit
Remove from us the sin that so inhibits
Light up our lives with the beauty of holiness
Touch us again – for You long to bless

You our Father and magnificent King
We bow before You, to You we cling
You are our Rock and our Refuge strong
We are Your children, to You we belong

Drive the enemy away with the breath of Your mouth
We have nothing, You are more than Enough
You send Your angels to lift us and bear us
Your lifegiving Word strengthens and cheers us

We praise You forever, God above
Humbly we crave Your arms of Love
To know Your voice of calm within
At Calvary You bore our weight of sin

Beautiful Jesus, pure and holy
You live on high, yet dwell with the lowly
May we be channels of Your love and grace
As You move among us in this place

Behold! I Make All Things New

(Inspired by Revelation 21: 5)

Behold I make all things new
Behold, I make, I make all things new
You are My children and I love you
I want to grow you in My love
Take off your garments of sin and sorrow
Put on My robe of righteousness
Clothed in My robe you are My jewels
The sparkling diamonds in My crown

You are My own, My blessed possession
I bought and claimed you with My Blood
Now you are made My new creation
Rise up and walk in victory
For in My Name you have My power
And in My Name authority
Drive out the evil, go heal the sick
And you will see My Word is Truth

For men will rise and will be healed
As Kingdom Power flows through you
My Power flows when you are humble
And when you stoop to hear My Voice
Incline your ear, you stiff-necked people
Bend low to hear, soften your hearts
Oh, listen to Me! Do not reject Me
I long to touch and make you whole

I am uprooting from deep within you
Those things that seek to keep you bound
Be not astounded for I am shaking
Establishments and things of man
That what remains be pure and holy
My radiant Bride prepared for Me
For I am gathering from all the nations
My sheep far-flung in all the earth

I am the Shepherd, I am the Bridegroom
Take heed and watch, I'm coming soon
Remain alert, be found not sleeping
For you know not the time nor hour
But look around you, observe the signs
The Winnower comes, the Lord is nigh
The Spirit speaks, close not your ears
Look up and see the Morning Star

You Are God

You are the Son, You are the One
You are my King, my everything
Lord of all in Heaven and Earth
You are the Pearl of utmost worth

I give my life to You my Lord
Glorious Spirit, Living Word
Come fill me now, lift me again
Let Your Spirit overflow and reign
In all I think and do and say
Lord Jesus rule – and have Your way

You created me and You have planned
A purpose for me – I'm in Your hand
You knew the moment for my birth
And You gave Your life for me on earth
On a cruel Cross You bore my shame
My sin, my fear and all my pain

You died for me, You took my place
You bore the penalty of my disgrace
You left Your glory in Heaven to be
Born on earth as a small baby
Helpless, vulnerable, Gift from above
That we might know the Father's love

You lived amongst us, You laid Your life down
You exchanged Your glory for a crown
Of thorns – You shed Your Blood and died
And Your sacrifice has opened wide
The Way for mankind to enter in
To the heart of the Father, all sin forgiven

For Jesus You're Victor, You have won
The battle with Evil – and it is done
Through humble submission to Your Father's plan
Jesus You now sit at His right hand
All power and glory are in Your Name
And You're coming again on Earth to reign

My heart is forever grateful Lord
I am Your child and You are God!

It's All About You Lord

It's all about You Lord, it's all about You
Risen from the dead, our living Saviour
In knowing You we will live forever
Oh joy unspeakable, delight indescribable!
To know You Jesus is Life and Truth and Peace
All things are possible with You, God of Grace

How we need You each moment and every hour
Your Word of Wisdom, Your Word of Power
You lift our heads when we are down
You our Encourager, our Strength, our Crown
You the Music in our hearts
that fills our voice with praise
Knowing we are loved by You
throughout endless days

You our Morning Light, our Midday Sun,
our Evening Sunset, Lord
We would not be without You, Jesus
Anointed Living Word
You bear us high in storms of wind and rain
You set us firmly on the Rock of Faith again
You our Refuge in all distress
You our gentle whisper and sweet caress

Darkness must flee in the Light of Your Glory
Dispelling our fear, our guilt, our worry
You the Balm for our lonely aching heart
You our Comfort, You set us apart
As Your sons and daughters, You raise us to Heaven
By Mercy and Grace from the Father given

You Divine Healer of our soul
You pour in Your love and You make us whole
You reign on high, yet live with the lowly
You say "Be holy as I am holy"
You raise us up Lord, we give You our praise
We bow before You, God of all Grace

Celebrating the Tabernacle of the King

To tabernacle with the King
We lift our voice in praise and sing
To Him Who reigns upon the Throne
Who calls us all His very own

Bought with His Blood on Calvary's Tree
His love so great for you and me
He took our sin upon Himself
He rose in victory over death

Precious gift of God to us
There's no-one like Christ Jesus
The least we now can do is bring
Our hearts, our lives, our love to Him

We join our hands, we dance, we pray
United on this joyful day
To tabernacle with our King
In worship do we honour Him

The New Jerusalem

Adorning the New Jerusalem
Rainbow colours of flashing gem

First foundation – Jasper's hue

In the second Sapphire blue

Layer three Chalcedony's gleam

Fourth is Emerald's depth of green

Sardonyx shines in layer fifth

Sardius' ruby-red is sixth

Seventh shines yellow Chrysolite

Next is Beryl's blue-green light

Golden Topaz number nine

Chrysoprase light-green next gives shine

Orange-red Jacinth last but one

Purple Amethyst makes the crown

Twelve Foundation Stones shine out
Praise to Jesus! Hosanna shout!
He is the Pearl of utmost worth
He is the Lord of Heaven and Earth!

Messiah King

The beauty and peace of sunlight dawning
The cool crisp air of the new morning
Blackbird busy on the grass
Tilting his head to hear worms pass

Fluffy white clouds sail above
In the endless blue of God's great love
Creator making all things new
Lord we bow and worship You

Thank You God for loving me
For sending Jesus to Calvary
Only He could make the sacrifice
To atone for my sin He paid the price

His life laid down that I might live
His glory exchanged that He might give
The gift of freedom to love Him always
To bow my heart in endless praise

Only One God for men to adore
Only One God Who chose to pour
Upon mankind His mercy and grace
To shine upon us His lovely face

Help men to choose Your way O Lord
To fall in love with Your living Word
To resist temptation and turn from sin
To receive You Lord and enter in

To the life You planned from Eternity
To live with You our Destiny
King of our hearts for ever Lord
We thank You Lord for the Living Word

Jesus Messiah King of Glory
Only You are forever Worthy
Jesus the Life the Truth the Way
I give You my life anew this day

Alphabet of the King

Awe-inspiring
Beautiful
Captivating
Deity

Everlasting
Faithful
Glorifying
Holy

Inimitable
Justifying
Kneeling
Lowly

Magnificent
Noble
Omnipotent
Purity

Quintessential
Royal
Sanctifying
Truly

Unique
Victorious
Worthy
"X"cellent

Yahweh!
Zion's King!

Forgiveness

Hearts are heavy, worn down with care,
Hurt and wounded by reckless words;
Painfully beating through the day,
Sorrowing and tearful in the night.
Increased burdens add weight to weight;
The daily journey hard to bear.
Where is joy and where is hope? Hearts cry silently,
Fearful of not finding any answer.

Till One knocks gently: "Will you let Me in?
Only I can release you from pain and sin.
I have known you from the beginning of time,
I have watched and waited through the years –
Close, so close to your hurt and tears,
Holding you when you knew Me not,
Carrying you when you could not go on;
All your answer is in Me.

I have the Master Plan for your life;
I hold your heart and soul, you are made in My image,
Created beautiful for Me, designed with perfect care and art.
When you let Me in I fill your heart
That you may live released and free,
Fulfilling all I have designed you to be.
The weights of years and all your tears
Are washed away in the forgiveness of Calvary.

My Blood has wrought entrance to the Father's Throne,
Has created the way to live forever free –
That where I am, there you may be also
As you pass from Death to Life in Eternity with Me.
This is Joy, this is Hope, this is Love; believe in Me –
I am the true Light that has come into the world,
I have conquered Death and Sin, I have been the sacrificial Lamb –
Forgiveness for all Time

True Light

When true Light comes into our soul,
Illuminating the hidden corners of our human anguish,
Where areas untouched, unrevealed for years
Are laid bare in the searchlight of God's mercy –
Then it is that deep burdens rise to the surface,
Break through with weeping and relief,
Releasing their bands of control and shame,
Submitted at last to the Saviour's Name.

That Name! Oh, the glory of the Name of Jesus!
Setting us free from every bondage of the sin of generations
So that we step into the fresh, new world of God's Kingdom –
In the world still, but not of it – for all has changed!
Creation looks bright and new, vibrant in colours of every hue.
Scales have fallen from our eyes and now we see light
in His true Light,
Revealing His Nature, His vast abounding Love and Mercy,
His boundless Salvation making us whole.

Our hearts are full, our joy a spring of everlasting hope in Jesus,
The Light that lights up every man, woman and child
Created and fashioned in His image to reflect the Lord,
To be a vessel individually indwelt by His Spirit,
Fulfilling the Master's design to light up the souls of all people,
To lift them from the darkness, to reconcile them to His heart,
To fill them with His Light and Beauty, His Love and Delight
That they too may see the power and glory of our soon-coming King!

The Rider On the White Horse

The shofar blows and rings within our being
Your coming is soon, the world weary and forlorn
Tempest-tossed, deceived, hopeless, downcast
Behold! The White Horse Rider with sounding horn
Summons all the earth to bow in worship
Before King Yeshua forever Victor crowned

About the Author

Joanna was born and brought up in Kenya, East Africa. She travelled widely as a young adult and later, when married to a nautical Captain, sailed with him to many distant places, which stretched her imagination and gave her many ideas for her poetry. Finally settling in New Zealand with her husband Tim, she continued to write in between bringing up two children, working part-time, and continuing to travel around the North and South Islands on family holidays.

Becoming a dedicated Christian in the early 1980s, her poetry took on a different focus. Her hope is that people will be encouraged and challenged in their own life journey, while recognising that all good and gracious gifts come from the hand of a loving God who has a specific purpose and plan for each one of us. The greatest gift of all to mankind has been the redemptive sacrifice of His Son Jesus Christ on the Cross at Calvary, rescuing us from the bondage of sin as we repent before our loving God and are thus "accepted in the Beloved."

Happily married for nearly 54 years till Tim died in 2018, Joanna now lives on the Kapiti Coast, where she continues to write and enjoy "anything to do with words"!

www.ingramcontent.com/pod-product-compliance
Lightning Source LLC
Chambersburg PA
CBHW062023290426
44108CB00024B/2762